Credits

Publisher:	Truly Hooked
Author:	Verity Castledine
Photography:	Meyrick Harris
Design and layout:	Meyrick Harris
Technical charts:	Meyrick Harris
Printers:	Bishops
Models:	Verity Castledine
	Nicola Nattrass
Sample knitters:	Gemma Watson
	Jo Aldridge
	Samantha Hinks
	Hayley Frye
	Helena Marsh

The Sock Drawer
Published by Truly Hooked 2016

ISBN:978-0-9955333-0-1
RRP £15.00
Second edition 2019

The Sock Drawer

Delilah 16

Arwen 22

Josephine 42

Cadena 48

Eleanor 70

Stitchionary 78

Introduction

Slipping your feet into the first pair of socks you've knitted for yourself, is a feeling of unbridled joy that, for me, has never gone away.

Admit it, you've all done the 'I made a sock' jig to yourself! Writing this collection of patterns has felt like that too and I'm delighted to be able to share them all with you. They're all deceptively simple, easy to follow and perfect for any experience level.

Be sure to check out the stitchionary at the back for help with anything that's unfamiliar.
Happy sock knitting!
Love Verity

Francis

Perfect for men or women, this simple pattern creates an attractive texture, and is a brilliant first step up from a basic sock. The short row heel makes it quick to knit, however you can work a regular heel flap if you prefer.

Francis

Materials:

1 skein EasyKnits Deeply Wicked in Merlot (100% superwash merino 4 ply, 425m per 100g)
2.5mm 9" mini circular needle or a longer cable for magic loop.
stitch markers

To begin:

CO 64 using a long tail cast on. Join in the round taking care not to twist the stitches

Ribbing:

* k2, p2 * to end of row, place marker.
Repeat for 12-20 rows.

Reading from the bottom right hand corner of the chart, work across the bottom row to establish pattern, and repeat it until the end of the row. Continue working from the chart, or follow the written instructions below:

Written pattern:

R1: * yo, ssk, k4, p2 * repeat to end of row
R2: * k1, yo, ssk, k3, p2 * repeat to end of row
R3: * k2, yo, ssk, k2, p2 * repeat to end of row
R4: * k3, yo, ssk, k1, p2 * repeat to end of row
R5: * k4, yo, ssk, p2 * repeat to end of row
R6: * k6, p2 * repeat to end of row
R7: repeat row 6
R8: repeat row 6

Repeat pattern 8-10 times down the leg

To work a short row heel (with no wraps):

With RS facing, work the heel across 32 stitches, leaving the remaining 32 unworked
sl 1, k across and leave last st unworked, turn,
sl 1, p across and leave last st unworked, turn,
sl 1, k across and leave last TWO st unworked, turn,
sl 1, p across and leave last TWO st unworked, turn,
sl 1, k across and leave last THREE st unworked, turn,

Continue in this way until you have 10 unworked st either side of your working st

RS: sl 1, k to 1 st before the gap, sl next st onto RH needle, pick up the bar running between the gap and put it on the RH needle. Insert LH needle through the front of the 2 stitches on the RH needle and k2tog as if doing a ssk decrease. Turn.

WS: sl1, and p to 1 st before the gap, sl next st onto RH needle, pick up the bar running between the gap and put it on the RH needle. Insert LH needle through the back of the 2 stitches on the RH needle p2tog. Turn.

Continue this way until you have closed all the gaps and you have 32 st on your heel.

Note: You may want to pick up and decrease an extra stitch either side to ensure there are no gaps

With RS facing, place marker and knit in row 1 of pattern across the top of the sock (32st), place marker and knit across the sole of the foot.

Continue to work in pattern until foot measures approx. 1.5-2 inches less than your foot length.

For the toe:

R1: knit until three stitches before your first marker, k2tog, k1, slip marker
k1, ssk, knit until three stitches before next marker, k2tog, k1, slip marker
k1, ssk, knit to end of round.
R2: Knit every stitch.

Repeat these two rows until you have 12 stitches between each marker and use Kitchener stitch to graft the toe closed.

Repeat for the second sock, sew in your ends and block gently.

Chart:

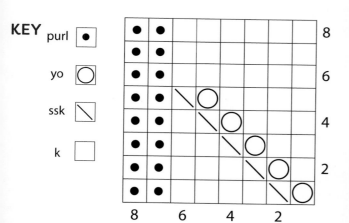

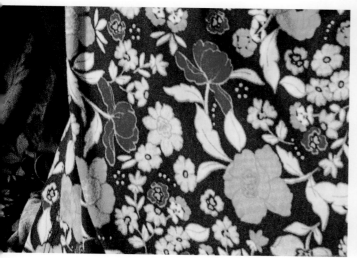

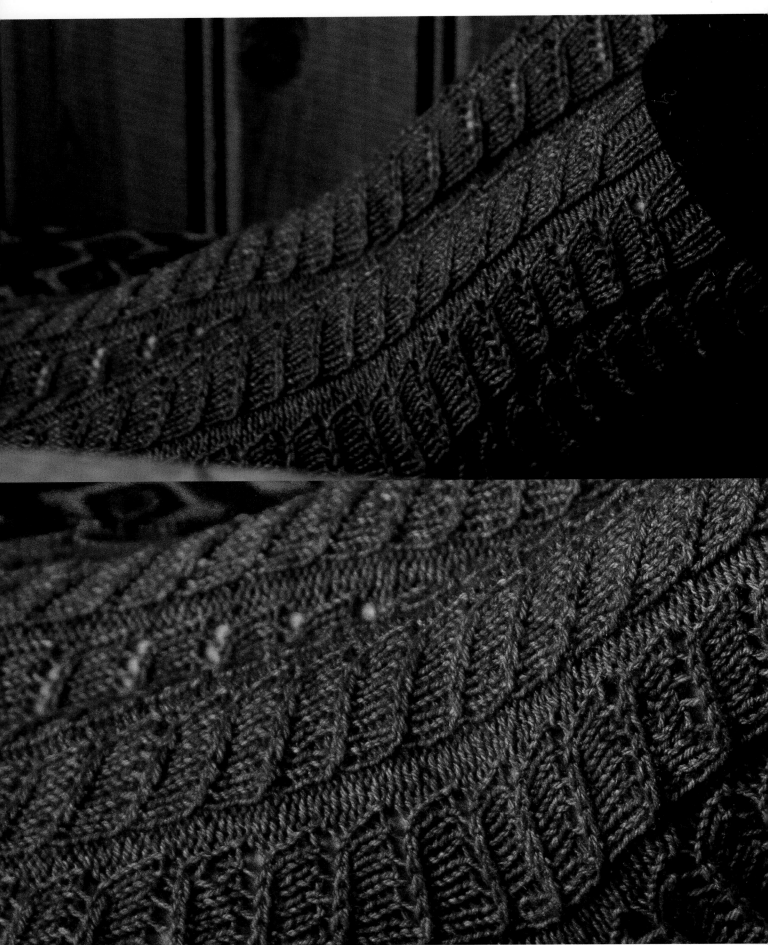

Delilah

With its simple four row repeat, and the added interest of twisted stitches, Delilah is a wonderful introduction to lace knitting.

Delilah

Materials:

1 skein Truly Hooked high twist mcn sock in Dusky Pink (80% superwash merino, 10% nylon, 10% cashmere, 365m per 100g)
2.5mm 9" mini circular needle or desired cable length for magic loop
stitch markers

To begin:

CO 60 (72) st using a long tail cast on. Join yarn into the round, taking care not to twist your stitches. Place a marker at the start of your round, and slip this each time you pass it.

Ribbing:

*p1, [k1 tbl, p1] twice, k3, p1, k3 * repeat * to * to the end of the row.
repeat this row a total of 12 times.

Working from the bottom right of the chart, repeat chart 5 (6) times around the sock. Continue to work in pattern and repeat 12-16 times until leg is desired length. The written pattern is also provided.

Written Pattern:

R1: * p1, [k1 tbl, p1] twice, k1, k2tog, yo, k1, yo, ssk, k1* repeat to end
R2: * p1, [k1 tbl, p1] twice, k7 * repeat to end
R3: * p1, [k1 tbl, p1] twice, k2tog, yo, k3, yo, ssk* repeat to end
R4: * p1, [k1tbl, p1] twice, k7 * repeat to end.

Heel:

Turn, and work on the next 30 st leaving remaining 30 (42) unworked on your needle
WS: sl 1, p to end of row, turn
RS: * sl 1, k1 * turn

Repeat these two rows 16 times in total (32 rows) and the WS row once more

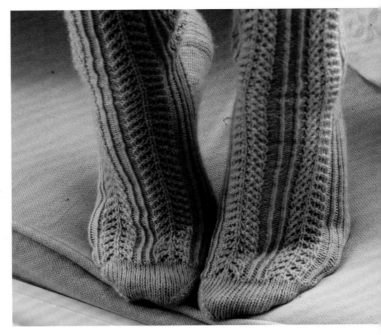

To turn the heel,

sl 1, k 16 (18), ssk, k1, turn
sl 1, p 5, p2tog, p1, turn

R1: sl 1, k until you reach the 'gap', ssk, k1, turn
R2: sl 1, p until you reach the gap, p2tog, turn.

Repeat R1 and R2 until you cannot decrease anymore and finish on a RS row.

Gusset:

Pick up and knit 17 (19) st along the left side of your heel flap, place marker and work row 1 of pattern across the instep (this is the 30 (42) stitches that were previously left unworked), place marker, pick up and knit 17 (19) st down right side of heel flap. Knit to first marker.

Knit a full round working in pattern across the instep.

R1: Knit in pattern across instep , slip marker, k1, ssk, k to 3st before marker, k2tog, k1
R2: Knit a full round working in pattern across instep.

Repeat rows 1 and 2, working in pattern on the instep until you have 30st between your markers on the sole.

Repeat the pattern down the foot until it measures 1.5-2 inches shorter than the desired length.

For the toe:

R1: k until 3 st before your first marker, k2tog, k1, slip marker

k1, ssk, k until 3 st before next marker, k2tog, k1, slip marker

k1, ssk, k to end of round.

R2: K every stitch.

Repeat these two rows until you have 12 stitches between each marker and use Kitchener stitch to graft the toe closed.

Repeat for the second sock, sew in your ends and block gently.

Delilah

Chart

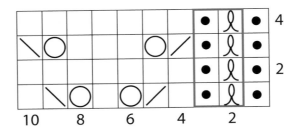

KEY

k	☐
purl	•
yo	◯
ssk	╲
k2tog	╱
pattern repeat	☐
ktbl	ℓ

Arwen

Striking, yet simple, Arwen combines two mock cable designs with slight ribbing to add stretch. A quick knit, for a classy sock.

Arwen

Materials:
2 skiens Socks Yeah! In Kunzite (75% superwash merino, 25% nylon, 212m per 50g)
2.5mm 9" mini circular needles or desired cable length for magic loop
stitch markers

To begin:
C0 60 (75) using a long tail cast on. Join in the round, taking care not to twist your stitches.

Ribbing:
* p1, k6, p1, k6, p1 * repeat to end, place marker after your first round.
Repeat this row 3 more times

Following chart A from the bottom right, work row 1 to establish pattern. Continue working in pattern and repeat the chart 5 times in total. Written instructions are also provided.

Pattern A:
R1: * p1, yo, k1, ssk, k3, p1, k3, k2tog, k1, yo, p1 * repeat to end of row
R2: * p1, k1, yo, k1, ssk, k2, p1, k2, k2tog, k1, yo, k1, p1 * repeat to end of row
R3: * p1, k2, yo, k1, ssk, k1, p1, k1, k2tog, k1, yo, k2, p1 * repeat to end of row
R4: * p1, k3, yo, k1, ssk, p1, k2tog, k1, yo, k3, p1 * repeat to end of row
R5: * p1, k6, p1, k6, p1 * repeat to end of row
R6: as row 5

Reading from the bottom right of chart B, work row 1 to establish pattern and continue working in the chart. Repeat the full chart a total of 5 times. Written instructions are provided.

Pattern B:
R1: * p1, k3, k2tog, k1, yo, p1, yo, k1, ssk, k3, p1 * repeat to end of row
R2: * p1, k2, k2tog, k1, yo, k1, p1, k1, yo, k1, ssk, k2, p1 * repeat to end of row
R3: * p1, k1, k2tog, k1, yo, k2, p1, k2, yo, k1, ssk, k1, p1 * repeat to end of row
R4: * p1, k2tog, k1, yo, k3, p1, k3, yo, k1, ssk, p1 * repeat to end of row
R5: * p1, k6, p1, k6, p1 * repeat to end of row
R6: as row 5

Heel:
Turn, and work on the next 30 st leaving remaining 30 (45) unworked on your needle
WS: sl 1, p6, k1, p6, k2, p6, k1, p7, turn
RS: sl 1, k6, p1, k6, p2, k6, p1, k7, turn

Repeat these two rows 16 times in total (32 rows) and the WS row once more

To turn the heel,
sl 1, k 16, ssk, k1, turn
sl 1, p 5, p2tog, p1, turn

R1: sl 1, k until you reach the 'gap', ssk, k1, turn
R2: sl 1, p until you reach the gap, p2tog, turn.
Repeat R 1 and 2 until you cannot decrease anymore and finish on a RS row.

Gusset:

Pick up and knit 17 (19) st along the left side of your heel flap, place marker and work row 1 of pattern A across the instep, place marker, pick up and knit 17 (19) st down right side of heel flap. Knit to first marker.

Knit a full round working in pattern A across the instep.

R1: Knit pattern across instep, slip marker, k1, ssk, k to 3st before marker, k2tog, k1
R2: Knit a full round working pattern A across instep.

Repeat rows 1 and 2, working in pattern A on the instep, until you have 30st between your markers on the sole.

Repeat the pattern A down the foot 5 times in total, and then repeat row 6 only until your foot measures 1.5-2 inches shorter than the desired length.

For the toe:

As you work the toe, not including the first 3 st after the markers, and last 3 st before the markers, continue to work row 6 of the pattern by knitting all the knit stitches, and purling all the purls.

R1: knit until three stitches before your first marker, k2tog, k1, slip marker
k1, ssk, knit until three stitches before next marker, k2tog, k1, slip marker
k1, ssk, knit to end of round.
R2: Knit every stitch.

Repeat these two rows until you have 12 stitches between each marker and use Kitchener stitch to graft the toe closed.

Repeat for the second sock, sew in your ends and block gently.

Charts

A

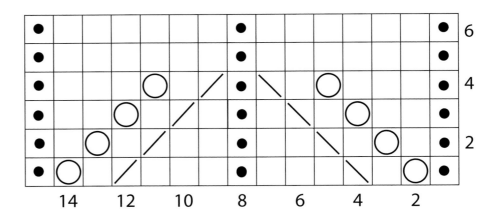

KEY

k ☐

purl ⊡

yo ◯

ssk ◺

k2tog ◿

B

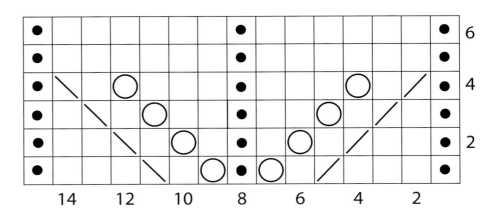

Rhian

Twisted ribbing and a mock cable design combine to create a striking but simple sock. Each one is worked differently so they mirror one another. The eye of partridge heel adds a different texture than a regular heel flap.

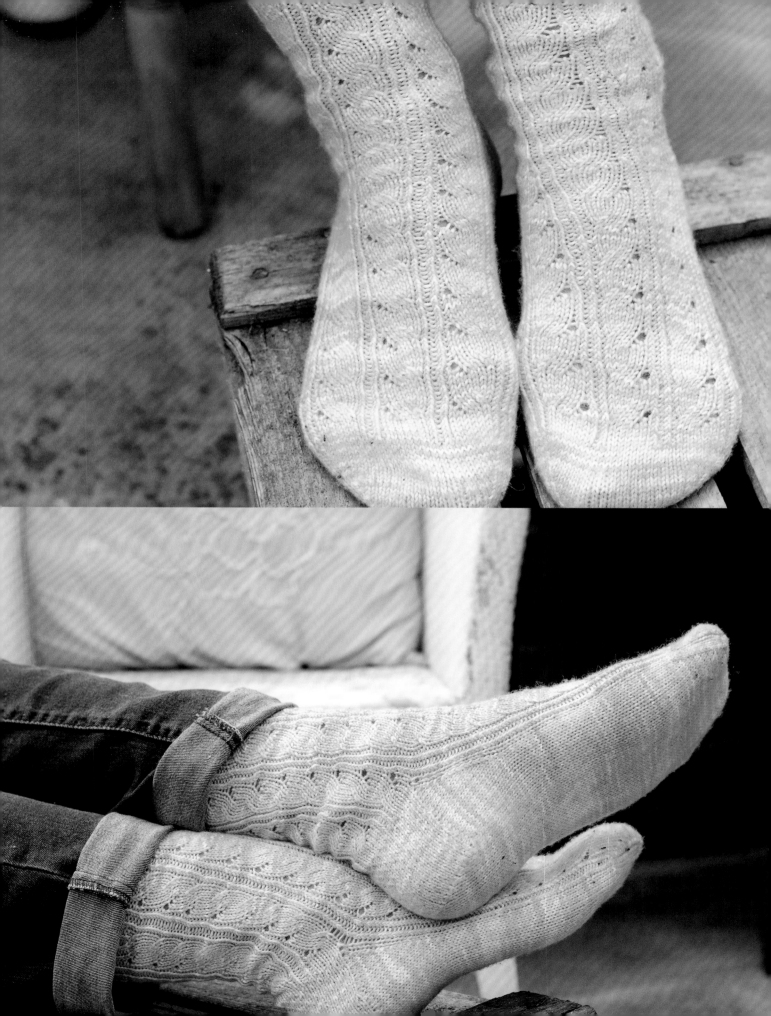

Rhian

Materials:

1 skein of Truly Hooked standard sock in 'Yellow Jersey' (75% superwash merino, 25% nylon, 425m per 100g)
2.5mm 9" mini circular needles or longer cable for magic loop
stitch markers

To begin:

CO 60 (70, 80) st using the long tail cast on.
Join in the round, taking care not to twist your stitches.

Ribbing:

R1: * k1 tbl, p1 * repeat to end of round. Place marker and continue to work in the round.
Repeat 9 more times.

Reading from the bottom right of the chart, work row 1 of chart A 6 (7, 8) times to complete the round. Continue working the chart down the leg of your sock.

Written pattern:

R1: * [k1 tbl, p1] twice, yo, k2, ssk, k2 * repeat to end of round
R2: * [k1 tbl, p1] twice, k1, yo, k2, ssk, k1 * repeat to end of round

R3: * [k1 tbl, p1] twice, k2, yo, k2, ssk * repeat to end of round
R4 – 7: * [k1, tbl, p1] twice, p1, k6 * repeat to end of round.

Continue working in pattern until you have repeated it 8-10 times.
Turn your work to begin the heel, working across 30 (36, 40) st.

To make the Eye of Partridge heel flap:

R1 (ws): sl 1, p to end of row, turn,
R2 (rs): * sl 1, k1 * repeat to end of row, turn,
R3 (ws): sl 1, p to end of row, turn
R4 (rs): sl 1, k2, * sl 1, k 1 * repeat to end of row, k last st. turn,

Repeat rows 1-4 eight times in total fin shing with a further R1. Turn your work so the right side is facing.

To turn the heel:

R1: Sl 1, k 16 (19, 21), ssk, k1, turn leaving remaining st unworked,
R2: sl1, p5, p2tog, p1, turn leaving remaining st unworked,
R3: sl 1, k to 1 st before the 'gap', ssk to close the gap, k1, turn leaving remaining st unworked,

R4: sl 1, p to 1 st before the 'gap', p2tog to close the gap, p1, turn leaving remaining st unworked,

Repeat rows 3 and 4 until there are no unworked st left, finish on a RS row. Do not turn,

Gusset:

Pick up and knit along the left side of your heel flap, place marker and work row 1 of pattern across the instep, place marker, pick up and knit down right side of heel flap. Knit to first marker.

NOTE: for medium, you will need to work an extra [k1tbl, p1] twice after you have repeated the pattern chart a total four times across your instep for every row down the foot

Knit a full round working in pattern across the instep.

R1: Knit pattern across instep, slip marker, k1, ssk, k to 3st before marker, k2tog, k1

R2: Knit a full round working pattern across instep.

Repeat rows 1 and 2, working in pattern on the instep until you have 30 st between your markers on the sole.

Repeat the pattern down the foot until it measures 1.5-2 inches shorter than the desired length.

For the toe:

R1: knit until three stitches before your fi st marker, k2tog, k1, slip marker
k1, ssk, knit until three stitches before next marker, k2tog, k1, slip marker
k1, ssk, knit to end of round.

R2: Knit every stitch.

Repeat these two rows until you have 12 stitches between each marker and use Kitchener stitch to graft the toe closed.

Repeat for the second sock, sew in your ends and block gently.

If you wish to reverse sock 2, work it in the same way as sock 1, but with the following instructions in place of the ribbing and chart A.

Ribbing:

*p1, k1tbl * for a total of 10 rows

Chart B:

R1: * k2, k2tog, k2, yo, [p1, k1tbl] twice * repeat to end of round

R2: * k1, k2tog, k2, yo, k1, [p1, k1tbl] twice * repeat to end of round

R3: * k2tog, k2, yo, k2, [p1, k1tbl] twice * repeat to end of round

R4-7: * k6, [p1, k1tbl] twice * repeat to end of round

Rhian

Charts:

A:

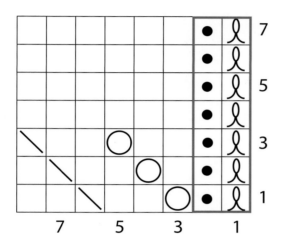

B:

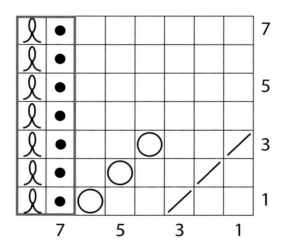

Tricia

Inspired by the twisting passionflower growing up the trellis outside my late grandmothers house, Tricia has a simple cable and lace repeat, and is perfect for introducing new skills to your sock knitting.

Tricia

Materials:
1 skein of Truly Hooked standard sock
(75% superwash merino/25% nylon, 425m per 100g)
in Pistachio
2.5mm 9" mini circular needles, or longer cable for
magic loop
2 stitch markers

To begin:
CO 64 (72) using the long tail cast on. Join in the
round taking care not to twist your stitches.

Ribbing:
 * p2(3), k4, p2 (3), k3, p2, k6, p2, k3, p2 (3), k4, p2
(3) * repeat once more.

Then repeat this row 9 more times for a total of 10
rounds. You may wish to place a marker both at the
start of the round, and after the fi st 32 (36) stitches
to help you keep your place.

Follow the chart, working from the bottom right to
establish pattern. Continue working in chart, or
follow written instruction below.

Written pattern:
R1: * p2 (3), C4F, p2 (3), k5, [k2tog, yo, k1] twice, k5,
p2 (3), c4b, p2 (3) * repeat to end
R2: * p2 (3), k4, p2 (3) , k16, p2 (3), k4, p2 (3) *
repeat to end
R3: * p2 (3), k4, p2 (3), k5, [yo, k1, k2tog] twice, k5,
p2 (3), k4, p2 (3) * repeat to end
R4: * p2 (3) , k4, p2 (3), k16, p2 (3), k4, p2 (3) *
repeat to end

Repeat these 4 rows 12-16 times until your leg is the
desired length. The heel is then worked across 32 (36)
stitches with the remaining 32 (36) left u worked for
now.

For the heel:
TURN to work on the wrong side
WS: sl 1, k1 (2), p4, k2 (3), p16, k2, (3) p4, k2 (3) turn
(32, 36 st worked)
RS: sl 1 wyif, p1 (2), k4, p2 (3), k16, p2 (3), k4, p2 (3),
turn (32, 36 st worked)

Repeat these 2 rows a total of 16 times (32 rows) and the
WS row once more so you fin sh with the RS row facing
you.

To turn the heel:
With RS facing,
sl 1, k17 (19) , ssk, k1 turn
sl 1, p6, p2tog, p1, turn

R1: sl 1, k to 1st before the the gap, ssk to close the gap,
k1, turn
R2: sl 1, p to 1st before the gap, p2tog, p1, turn

Repeat rows 1 and 2 until you cannot decrease across
the gap anymore & fin sh on a RS row.

Gusset:
Pick up and knit evenly along the left side f your heel
flap, place marker and work row 1 of pattern across the
instep, place marker, pick up and knit evenly down right
side of heel flap. Knit to fi st marker

Knit a full round working in pattern across the instep.

R1: Knit pattern across instep, slip marker, k1, ssk, k to
3st before marker, k2tog, k1
R2: Knit a full round working pattern across instep.

Continue working in pattern, repeating rows 1 and 2
until you have 32 (36) stiches between your markers on
the bottom of the foot. The top of the foot should always
stay at 32 (36) stitches.

Continue in pattern until your foot is approx
1.5-2inches shorter than your desired length.

For the toe:

R1: knit until three stitches before your first marker, k2tog, k1, slip marker
k1, ssk, knit until three stitches before next marker, k2tog, k1, slip marker
k1, ssk, knit to end of round.
R2: Knit every stitch.

Repeat these two rows until you have 12 stitches between each marker and use Kitchener stitch to graft the toe closed.

Repeat for the second sock, sew in your ends and block gently.

Tricia
Charts:

Small

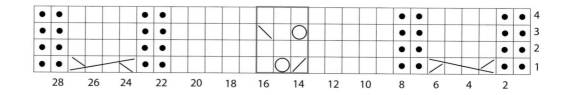

28 26 24 22 20 18 16 14 12 10 8 6 4 2

Large

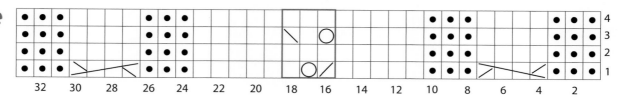

32 30 28 26 24 22 20 18 16 14 12 10 8 6 4 2

KEY

k   purl   yo   ssk   k2tog   C4B   C4F

Josephine

Delicate lace adorns this pretty sock which is easy to memorise and great for picking up and putting down. With ribbing built into the sock, this cuffless design begins almost from the very top creating a different look.

Josephine

Materials:

1 skein Truly Hooked standard sock in Candy Floss (75% superwash merino, 25% nylon, 425m per 100g)
2.5mm 9" circular needles, or longer cable for magic loop
2 stitch markers

To begin:

CO 64 st using a long tail cast on. Join in the round taking care not to twist the stitches.

Set up row:

* p1, k3, p1, k6, p1, k3, p1 * repeat to end of row, join work in the round and place marker. Repeat this row three more times.

Reading from the bottom right corner of the chart, knit row 1 of the chart twice around the sock. Continue following the chart to complete the pattern once. Working in pattern, repeat the chart 6 times in total. The written pattern is also provided

Written pattern:

R1: * p1, k1, yo, k2tog, p1, yo, k1, ssk, k3, [p1, k1, yo, k2tog, p1] twice, k3, k2tog, k1, yo, p1, k1, yo, k2tog, p1 * twice

R2: * p1, k3, p1, k1, yo, k1, ssk, k2, [p1, k3, p1] twice, k2, k2tog, k1, yo, k1, p1, k3, p1 * twice

R3: * p1, yo, ssk, k1, p1, k2, yo, k1, ssk, k1, [p1, yo, ssk, k1, p1] twice, k1, k2tog, k1, yo, k2, p1, yo, ssk, k1, p1 * twice

R4: * [p1, k3] twice, yo, k1, ssk, [p1, k3, p1] twice, k2tog, k1, yo, [k3, p1] twice, * twice

R5: p1, k1, yo, k2tog, p1, k4, yo, k2tog, [p1, k1, yo, k2tog, p1] twice, ssk, yo, k4, p1, k1, yo, k2tog, p1 * twice

R6: * p1, k3, p1, k6, [p1, k3, p1] twice, k6, p1, k3, p1 * twice

R7: * p1, yo, ssk, k1, p1, k6, [p1, yo, ssk, k1, p1] twice, k6, p1, k3, p1 * twice

R8: repeat row 6

R9: * p1, k1, yo, k2tog, p1, k6, [p1, k1, yo, k2tog, p1] twice, k6, p1, k1, yo, k2tog, p1 * twice

R10: repeat row 6

R11: repeat row 7

R12: repeat row 6

Heel flap

Turn and work across next 32 stitches only leaving remaining stitches unworked on the needle,

WS: sl 1, p3, k1, p6, k1, p3, k2, p3, k1, p6, k1, p3, k1, turn
RS: sl 1, k3, p1, k6, p1, k3, p2, k3, p1, k6, p1, k3, p1, turn

Repeat these 2 rows 15 times more and the WS row once more.

To turn the heel,
With RS facing,
sl 1, k17, ssk, k1 turn
p 1, p6, p2tog, p1, turn

R1: sl 1, k to 1 st before the the gap, ssk to close the gap, k1, turn
R2: sl 1, p to 1 st before the gap, p2tog, p1, turn

Repeat r1 and 2 until you have 19 st, finishing on a RS row.

Gusset:

Pick up and knit 17 st along the left side of your heel flap, place marker and work row 9 of pattern across the instep, place marker, pick up and knit 17 st down right side of heel flap. Knit to first marker (53 st)

Knit a full round working in pattern across the instep.

R1: Knit pattern across instep, slip marker, k1, ssk, k to 3st before marker, k2tog, k1
R2: Knit a full round working pattern across instep.

Repeat rows 1 and 2, working rows 9-12 of pattern on the instep until you have 32 st between your markers on both the instep and the sole.

Work rows 9-12 of pattern a total of 10 times on the foot (start counting from the round when you began to work on the instep) and then repeat row 12 only until your foot is 1.5-2 inches shorter than your desired length.

For the toe:

R1: knit until three stitches before your first marker, k2tog, k1, slip marker
k1, ssk, knit until three stitches before next marker, k2tog, k1, slip marker
k1, ssk, knit to end of round.
R2: Knit every stitch.

Repeat these two rows until you have 12 stitches between each marker and use Kitchener stitch to graft the toe closed.

Repeat for the second sock, sew in your ends and block gently.

Chart:

KEY

k ☐

purl ☐•

yo ☐◯

ssk ☐\

k2tog ☐/

pattern repeat ☐

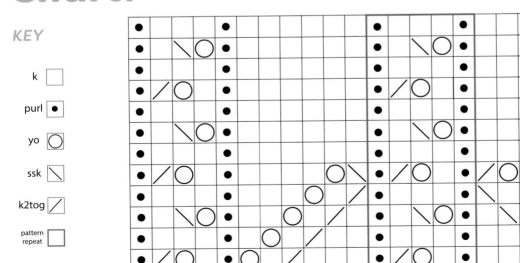

Cadena

Meaning 'chain', Cadena is a more complex cabled sock, with loops and twists and a dense twisting cuff. It requires a bit of concentration, but isn't a complicated knit.

Cadena

Materials:

1 skein Bellica Yarns Yak sock in Intense Blue (70% superwash merino, 20% nylon, 10% yak. 400m per 100g)

2.5mm 9" mini circular needle or desired cable length to do magic loop

stitch markers

Note: pattern is written for two sizes, worked across 64 (small) and 72 (large) stitches. Both patterns begin with 72 stitches. You may prefer to work the cabled cuff on a larger needle to give a little more stretch.

To begin:

Using a long tail or cable cast on, CO 72 st

* p2, k4 * repeat to end of row, join in the round taking care not to twist your work and place marker

Cabled cuff

R1: * p2, C4B * to end of row
R2: * p2, k4 * to end of row
R3 and 4: as row 2

Repeat these 4 rows a total of 5 times (20 rows)
For the smaller size only on the 20th row, k2tog every 9 stitches (64 st)

Working from the bottom right of the chart, work row 1 twice across the round You may wish to place a stitch marker after the first repeat to keep your place.

Continue working in pattern to the end of the chart, and repeat it once more. (twice if you prefer a longer leg). The written pattern is provided below:

Written pattern (L in brackets:

R1: * p2(4), k4, p6, k8, p6, k4, p2(4) * twice
R2: repeat row 1
R3: * p2(4), k4, p6, C4B, C4F, p6, k4, p2(4) * twice

R4: repeat row 1
R5: * p2(4), C4B, p6, k8, p6, C4F, p2(4) * twice
R6: repeat row 1
R7: * p2(4), k4, p6, C4F, C4B, p6, k4, p2(4) * twice
R8: repeat row 1
R9: repeat row 5
R10: as row 1
R11: repeat row 3
R12: as row 1
R13: as row 1
R14: as row 1
R15: repeat row 7
R16: as row 1

Heel flap

Turn, and work across the next 32 (36)st, leaving remaining 32 (36)st unworked on your needle
WS: sl1, k1(3), p4, k6, p8, k6, p4, k1(3), p1
RS: sl 1, p1(3), k4, p6, k8, p6, k4, p1(3), k1

Repeat these 2 rows 16 times in total and the WS row once more (33 rows)

To turn the heel,

With RS facing,
sl 1, k17(19), ssk, k1 turn
p1, p6, p2tog, p1, turn

R1: sl 1, k to 1st before the the gap, ssk to close the gap, k1, turn
R2: sl 1, p to 1st before the gap, p2tog, p1, turn

Repeat these two rows until you have 19(21)st, finish on a RS row.

Gusset:

Pick up and knit 17 (19) st along the left side of your heel flap, place marker and work row 1 of pattern across the instep, place marker, pick up and knit 17 (19) st down right side of heel flap. Knit to first marker (53 (55) st)

Knit a full round working row 2 of pattern across the instep.

R1: Knit in pattern across instep, slip marker, k1, ssk, k to 3st before marker, k2tog, k1
R2: Knit a full round working in pattern across instep.

Repeat rows 1 and 2, working in pattern on the instep until you have 32(36) st between your markers on both the instep and the sole. Total of 64 (72) st

Repeat the pattern four times on the foot and if needs be, repeat row 16 until your foot is 1.5-2 inches shorter than the desired length.

For the toe:
R1: knit until three stitches before your first marker, k2tog, k1, slip marker
k1, ssk, knit until three stitches before next marker, k2tog, k1, slip marker
k1, ssk, knit to end of round.
R2: Knit every stitch.

Repeat these two rows until you have 12 stitches between each marker and use Kitchener stitch to graft the toe closed.

Repeat for the second sock, sew in your ends and block gently.

Cadena

Charts:

Small

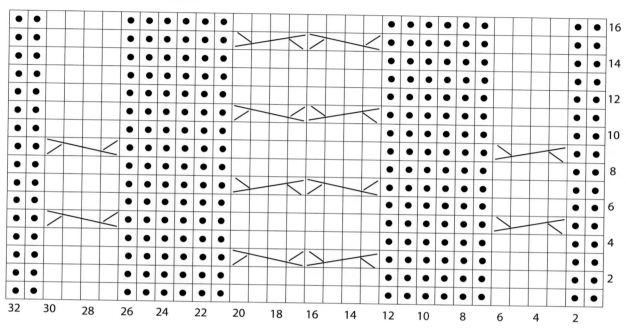

KEY

k	purl	C4B	C4F

Large

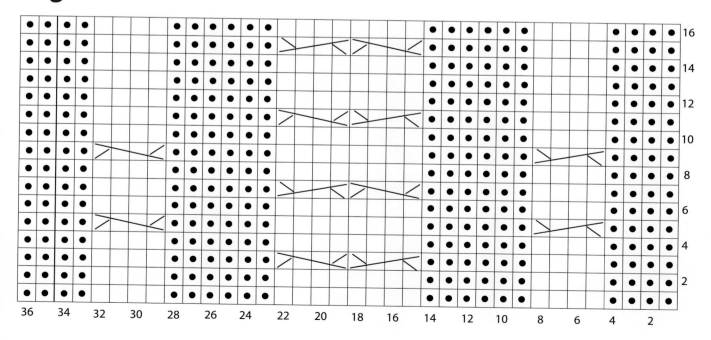

Elendil

Inspired by the mystical Elvish lands, the twisted ribbing, leaf like lace, and moss stitch armoured toe reflect the strong character of these mythical beings. Its cuffless design gives the illusion of never ending vines.
The socks are mirrored and each worked from separate charts.

Elendil

Materials:

1 skein Bellica Yarns high twist MCN sock in Radioactive (80% superwash merino, 10% nylon, 10% cashmere. 365m per 100g)
2.5mm 9" mini circular needles, or desired cable length for magic loop
stitch markers

To begin:

CO 60 st using a long tail cast on. Join to to work in the round taking care not to twist your stitches.

Set up row:

* p1, k5, p1, k1tbl, p1, k1tbl * to end of row. Place marker and repeat this row once more. You may also wish to place a marker after the fi st 30 stitches to help you keep your place.

Reading from the bottom right corner, work row 1 of chart A twice around the sock to establish pattern. Continue to work in chart. The written instructions are also provided.

Pattern A:

R1: * p1, yo, k1, ssk, k2, [p1, k1 tbl] twice *
R2: * p1, k1, yo, k1, ssk, k1, [p1, k1 tbl] twice *
R3: * p1, k2, yo, k1, ssk, [p1, k1 tbl] twice *
R4: * p1, k5, [p1, k1 tbl] twice *
R5: as row 4 p1, k5, [p1, k1 tbl] twice *
R6: * p1, k2, k2tog, k1, yo, [p1, k1 tbl] twice *
R7: * p1, k1, k2tog, k1, yo, k1, [p1, k1 tbl] twice *
R8: * p1, k2tog, k1, yo, k2, [p1, k1 tbl] twice *
R9: as row 4 * p1, k5, [p1, k1 tbl] twice *
R10: as row 4 * p1, k5, [p1, k1 tbl] twice *

Repeat pattern a total of 6 times on the leg.

Heel:

Turn, and work on the next 30 st leaving remaining 30 unworked on your needle

WS: sl 1, k1, p1tbl, k1 *p5, k1, [p1tbl,k1]* twice, rep from *to* once more, p5 k1
RS: sl 1, * k5, p1 [k1 tbl, p1] twice * repeat *to* once more, k5,p1, k1tbl, p1, k1tbl

Repeat these two rows 16 times in total (32 rows) and the WS row once more

To turn the heel,

sl 1, k 16, ssk, k1, turn
sl 1, p 5, p2tog, p1, turn

R1: sl 1, k to 1st before the gap, ssk to close the gap, k1, turn
R2: sl 1, p to 1st before the gap, p2tog, p1, turn

Repeat R1 and 2 until you cannot decrease anymore and finish on a RS row.

Gusset:

Pick up and knit 17 st along the left side of your heel flap, place marker and work row 1 of pattern across the instep, place marker, pick up and knit 17st down right side of heel flap. Knit to fi st marker.

Knit a full round working pattern as set across the instep

R1: Knit in pattern across instep, slip marker, k1, ssk, k to 3st before marker, k2tog, k1
R2: Knit a full round working pattern A across instep.
Repeat rows 1 and 2, working in pattern A on the instep until you have 30st between your markers on both the instep and the sole.

This sections ends with a row 3. Continue to work rows 4 - 10 with no decreases to complete the pattern a total of 3 times after the heel.

Working from bottom right of the chart, work row 1 of chart B across the instep to your marker, and then knit only on the sole stitches. Continue working chart B down the top of the foot. Written instructions are provided.

Pattern B.

R1: yo, ssk, k4, [p1, k1 tbl] twice, *p1, yo, k1, ssk, k2, [p1, k1 tbl]twice * REP *to* once more
R2: k1, yo, ssk, k3, [p1, k1 tbl] twice, *p1, k1 yo, k1, ssk, k1, [p1, k1 tbl] twice* rep from *to* once more
R3: p1, k1, yo, ssk, k2, [p1, k1 tbl] twice, *p1, k2 yo, k1, ssk, [p1, k1 tbl] twice * rep from *to* once more
R4: k1, p1, k1, yo, ssk, k1, [p1, k1 tbl] twice, *p1, k5, [p1, k1 tbl] twice * rep from *to* once more
R5: [p1, k1] twice, yo, ssk, [p1, k1 tbl] twice, *p1, k5, [p1, k1 tbl] twice * rep from *to* once more
R6: [k1, p1] twice, k1, yo, ssk, [k1 tbl, p1] twice, *p1, k2, k2tog, k1, yo, [p1, k1 tbl] twice * rep from *to* once more
R7: [p1, k1] three times, yo, ssk, p1, k1 tbl, *p1, k1, k2tog, k1, yo, k1 [p1, k1 tbl] twice * rep from *to* once more

R8: [k1, p1] three times, k1, yo, ssk, k1 tbl, *p1, k2tog, k1, yo, k2 [p1, k1 tbl] twice rep from *to* once more

R9: [p1, k1] four times, yo, skk, *p1, k5, [p1, k1 tbl] twice,* p1 repeat * to *

R10: [k1, p1] four times, k1, yo, skk, * k5, [p1, k1 tbl] twice * p1, repeat * to *

R11: [p1, k1] five times, yo, ssk, k4, [p1, k1tbl] twice, p1, yo, k1, ssk, k2, [p1, k1 tbl] twice

R12: [k1, p1] five times, k1,yo, ssk, k3, [p1, k1tbl] twice, p1, k1, yo, k1,ssk, k1, [p1, k1tbl] twice

R13: [p1, k1] six times, yo, ssk, k2, [p1, k1tbl] twice, p1, k2, yo, k1, ssk, [p1, k1 tbl] twice

R14: [k1, p1] six times, k1, yo, ssk, k1, [p1, k1tbl] twice, p1, k5, [p1, k1tbl] twice

R15: [p1, k1] seven times, yo, ssk, [p1, k1tbl] twice, p1, k5, [p1, k1tbl] twice

R16: [k1, p1] seven times, k1, yo ssk, [k1 tbl, p1] twice,k2, k2tog, k1, yo, [p1, k1 tbl] twice

R17: [p1, k1] eight times, yo, ssk, p1, k1 tbl, p1, k1, k2tog, k1, yo, k1, [p1, k1tbl] twice

R18: [k1, p1] eight times, k1,yo, ssk, k1 tbl, p1, k2tog, k1, yo, k2, [p1, k1tbl] twice

R19: [p1, k1] nine times, yo, ssk, p1, k5, [p1, k1tbl] twice

R20: [k1, p1] nine times, k1,yo, ssk, k5, [p1, k1tbl] twice,

R21: [p1, k1] ten times, yo, ssk, k4, [p1, k1tbl] twice,

R22: [k1, p1] ten times, k1,yo, ssk, k3, [p1, k1tbl] twice,

R23: [p1, k1] eleven times, yo, ssk, k2, [p1, k1tbl] twice,

R24: [k1, p1] eleven times, k1, yo, skk, k1, [p1, k1tbl] twice,

R25: [p1, k1] twelve times, yo, skk, [p1, k1tbl] twice,

R26: [k1, p1] twelve times, k1,yo, ssk, k1 tbl, p1, k1 tbl,

R27: [p1, k1] thirteen times, yo, ssk, p1, k1 tbl

R28: [k1, p1] thirteen times, k1,yo, ssk, k1 tbl

R29: [p1, k1] fourteen times, yo, ssk

R30: [k1, p1] fifteen times

R31: [p1, k1] fifteen times

Repeat row 30 and 31 until foot is 1.5-2 inches shorter than the desired length.

For the toe:

As you work the toe, not including the first 3 st after each marker and last 3 st before each marker, continue to work in moss stitch by knitting each purl and purling each knit from the previous row.

R1: k to 3 st before your fi st marker, k2tog, k1, slip marker k1, ssk, kto 3 st before next marker, k2tog, k1, slip marker k1, ssk, knit to end of round.

R2: Knit every stitch.

Repeat these two rows until you have 12 stitches between each marker and use Kitchener stitch to graft the toe closed.

For the second sock, work as the fi st until you reach the part that says 'follow pattern B, and instead, follow pattern C. Work the remainder of the foot and toe in the same way as sock 1.

Pattern C.

R1: *p1, yo, k1, ssk, k2, [p1, k1 tbl] twice* rep from*to* once more, p1, yo, k1, ssk, k2, p1, k1 tbl, k2tog, yo

R2: *p1, k1, yo, k1, ssk, k1, [p1, k1 tbl] twice,* rep from *to* once more, p1, k1 yo, k1, ssk, k1, p1, k2tog, yo, k1

R3: *p1, k2, yo, k1, ssk, [p1, k1 tbl] twice, * rep from *to* once more, p1, k2 yo, k1, ssk, k2tog, yo, k1, p1 **R4:** *p1, k5, [p1, k1 tbl] twice* rep from *to* once more p1, k4, k2tog, yo, k1, p1, k1

R5: *p1, k5 , [p1, k1 tbl] twice* rep from*to* once more, p1, k3, k2tog, yo, [k1, p1] twice

R6: *p1, k2, k2tog, k1, yo, [p1, k1 tbl] twice* rep from*-to* once more p1, k2, k2tog, yo, k1, [p1, k1] twice

R7: p1, k1, k2tog, k1, yo, k1 [p1, k1 tbl] twice * rep from *to* once more, p1, k1, k2tog, yo, [k1,p1] three times

R8: *p1, k2tog, k1, yo, k2 [p1, k1 tbl] twice * rep from *to* once more, p1, k2tog, yo, k1, [p1,k1] three times

R9: *p1, k5 , [p1, k1 tbl] twice* rep from*to* once more, k2tog, yo, [k1,p1] four times

R10: p1, k5 , [p1, k1 tbl] twice, p1, k5, p1, k1 tbl, p1, k2tog, yo, k1, [p1, k1] four times

R11: p1, yo, k1, ssk, k2, [p1, k1 tbl] twice, p1, yo, k1, ssk, k2, p1, k1 tbl, k2tog, yo, [k1, p1] fives times

R12: p1, k1, yo, k1, ssk, k1, [p1, k1 tbl] twice, p1, k1, yo, k1, ssk, k1, p1, k2tog, yo, k1, [p1, k1] fives times

R13: p1, k2, yo, k1, ssk, [p1, k1 tbl] twice, p1, k2, yo, k1, ssk, k2tog, yo, [k1, p1] six times

R14: p1, k5, [p1, k1 tbl] twice, p1, k4, k2tog, yo, k1, [p1, k1] six times

R15: p1, k5, [p1, k1 tbl] twice, p1, k3, k2tog, yo, [k1,p1],

seven times

R16: p1, k2, k2tog, k1, yo, [p1, k1 tbl] twice, p1, k2, k2tog, yo,k1, [p1, k1] seven times

R17: p1, k1, k2tog, k1, yo, k1, [p1, k1 tbl] twice, p1, k1, k2tog, yo, [k1, p1] eight times

R18: p1, k2tog, k1, yo, k2, [p1, k1 tbl] twice, p1, k2tog, yo, k1, [p1, k1] eight times

R19: p1, k5, p1, k1 tbl, p1, k1 tbl, k2tog, yo, [k1, p1] nine times

R20: p1, k5, p1, k1 tbl, p1, k2tog, yo, k1, [p1, k1] nine times

R21: p1, yo, k1, ssk, k2, p1, k1 tbl, k2tog, yo, [k1, p1] ten times

R22: p1, k1, yo, k1, ssk, k1, p1, k2tog, yo, k1, [p1, k1] ten times

R23: p1, k2, yo, k1, ssk, k2tog, yo, [k1, p1] eleven times

R24: p1, k4, k2tog, yo, k1. [p1, k1] eleven times

R25: p1, k3, k2tog, yo, [k1, p1] twelve times

R26: p1, k2, k2tog, yo, k1, [p1, k1] twelve times

R27: p1, k1, k2tog, yo, [k1, p1] thirteen times

R28: p1, k2tog, yo, k1, [p1, k1] thirteen times

R29: k2tog, yo, [k1, p1] fourteen times

R30: [p1, k1] fifteen times

R31: [k1, p1] fifteen times

Repeat row 30 and 31 until foot is 1.5-2 inches shorter than the desired length and follow instructions for the toe as given already.

Charts:

KEY

k	(blank box)
purl	•
yo	○
ssk	\
k2tog	/
ktbl	ℓ

A:

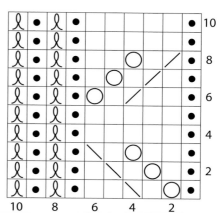

Elendil

B:

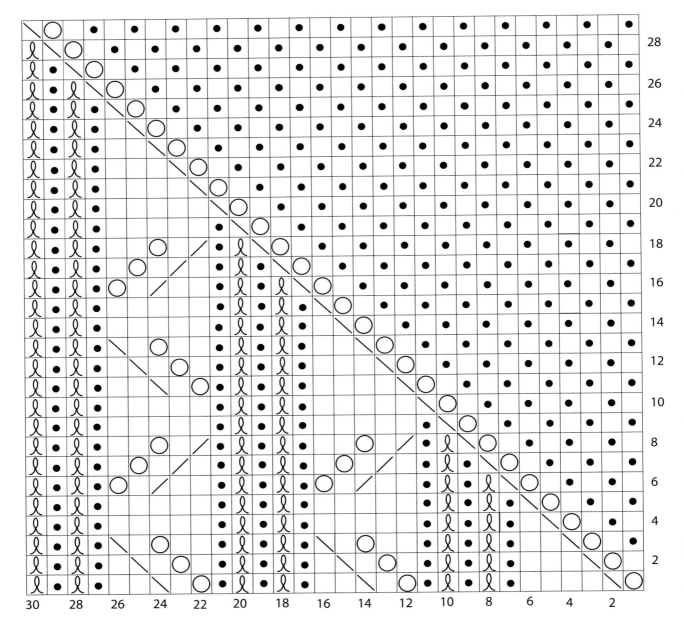

KEY

k	purl	yo	ssk	k2tog	ktbl

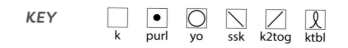

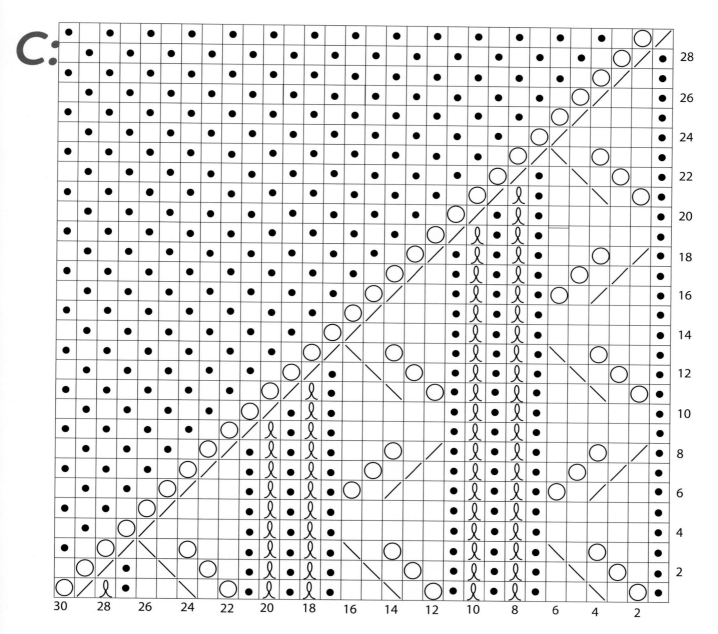

C:

28
26
24
22
20
18
16
14
12
10
8
6
4
2

30 28 26 24 22 20 18 16 14 12 10 8 6 4 2

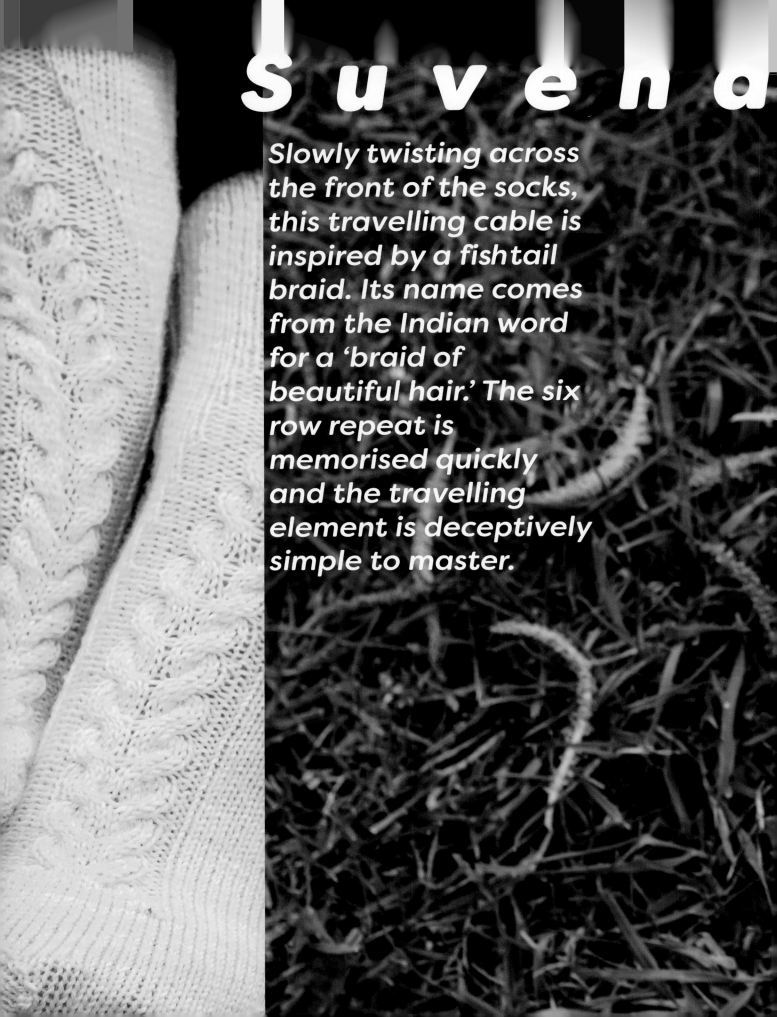

Suvena

Slowly twisting across the front of the socks, this travelling cable is inspired by a fishtail braid. Its name comes from the Indian word for a 'braid of beautiful hair.' The six row repeat is memorised quickly and the travelling element is deceptively simple to master.

Suvena

Materials:

1 skein of Truly Hooked standard sock in Sunshine Yellow (75% superwash merino, 25% nylon, 425m per 100g)
2.5mm 9" mini circular needles or desired cable length for magic loop
stitch markers

To begin:

CO 64 (72) using a long tail or cable cast on. Join work into the round taking care not to twist your stitches

Ribbing:

* p2 (3), k4, p4, k4, p2 (3) * repeat to end. Place a marker after the fi st 32 (36) stitches and another at the end of the round. This is important for working the main pattern.

Work a total of 10 rows of ribbing.

Working from the bottom right hand corner of the chart, knit row 1 and then knit to first marker to establish pattern, followed by * p2 (3), k4, p4, k4, p2 (3) * to end. Continue to work in chart, then knit to fi st marker, and in rib pattern as set to second marker. Written instructions are provided below.

Main pattern

R1: p2 (3) , C6F, C6B, p4 (6), knit to marker, * p2 (3), k4, p4, k4, p2 (3) * to end
R2: p2 (3) k12, p4 (6) knit to marker, * p2 (3), k4, p4, k4, p2 (3) * to end
R3: as row 2
R4: as row 2
R5: as row 2
R6: as row 2.

Repeat the pattern THREE times in total.

On the fourth repeat, KNIT 1 stitch at the start of each round, before working the pattern as written.

On the fifth repeat, KNIT 2 stitches at the start each round, before working the pattern as written.

On the sixth repeat, KNIT 3 stitches at the start of each round, before working the pattern as written.

Continue in this way, adding an extra stitch at the start of each round until you have worked 10 repeats.

To work the heel

Turn, and work across the next 32 (36) st leaving the remaining stitches unworked for now

WS: sl 1, k1 (2), [p4, k4] 3 times, p4, k2 (3), turn,
RS: sl 1 wyif, p1 (2), [k4, p4] 3 times, k4, p2 (3) turn

Repeat these 2 rows 15 times more and the WS row once more.

To turn the heel,

With RS facing,
sl 1, k17 (19), ssk, k1 turn
p1, p6, p2tog, p1, turn

R1: sl 1, k to 1st before the the gap, ssk to close the gap, k1, turn
R2: sl 1, p to 1st before the gap, p2tog, p1, turn

Repeat R1 and 2 until you cannot decrease across the gap anymore, fin shing on a RS row.

Gusset:

Note: the sole of the foot will now be worked in knit stitches only

Pick up and knit evenly along the left side of your heel flap, place marker and continue to work in pattern as set before across the instep, remembering to add an extra knit stitch at the start of the round. Place marker, pick up and knit evenly down right side of heel flap. Knit to first marker.

Knit a full round working in pattern as set across the instep.

R1: Knit pattern as set across instep, slip marker, k1, ssk, k to 3st before marker, k2tog, k1
R2: Knit a full round working pattern as set across instep.

Repeat rows 1 and 2, working the pattern as before on the instep remembering to add an extra knit stitch at the start of each round with each full repeat. Continue in this way until you have 32 (36) st between your markers on both the instep and the sole.

Knit in pattern until your cable has travelled across the sock, and your row ends with 4 (6) purl stitches before

the marker. Knit until your sock is 1.5-2inches shorter than your desired length.

For the toe:

R1: k until 3 st before your first marker, k2tog, k1, slip marker
k1, ssk, k until 3 st before next marker, k2tog, k1, slip marker k1, ssk, knit to end of round.
R2: Knit every stitch.

Repeat these two rows until you have 12 stitches between each marker and use Kitchener stitch to graft the toe closed.

For the second sock

Knit the ribbing as the first sock, then
R1: knit to 18 st before marker, p4 (6) , C6F, C6B, p2 (3), * p2 (3), k4, p4, k4, p2 (3) * to end
R2: knit to 18 st before marker, p4(6) k12, p2 (3) * p2 (3), k4, p4, k4, p2 (3) * to end
R3: as row 2
R4: as row
R5: as row 2
R6: as row 2.

Work the remainder of the sock in the same way as the first, BUT with each repeat, KNIT ONE LESS stitch before the cable section AND knit one
additional stitch after the cable section before the marker
Eg: on repeat 4
Knit to 17 st before the marker, p4 (6) C6F, C6B, p2 (3) k1, slip marker and work in rib to the end of the round.

On repeat 5, knit to 16 st before the marker, p4 (6) C6F, C6B, p2 (3) k2, slip marker and work in rib to the end of the round.

On repeat 6, knit to 15 st before the marker, p4 (6) C6F, C6B, p2 (3) k3, slip marker and work in rib to the end of the round.

Continue in this way until you have worked 10 repeats, then work the remainder of the sock in the same way as sock 1, ensuring you continue the
pattern as set on the instep of the foot.

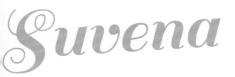

Suvena

Charts:

Small

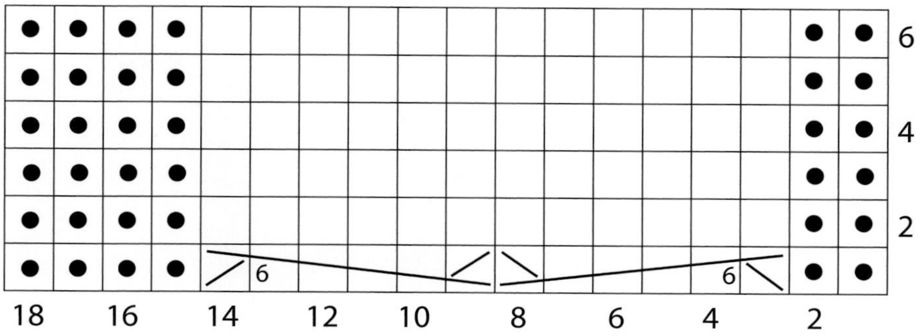
6
4
2
6
6
18
16
14
12
10
8
6
4
2

Large

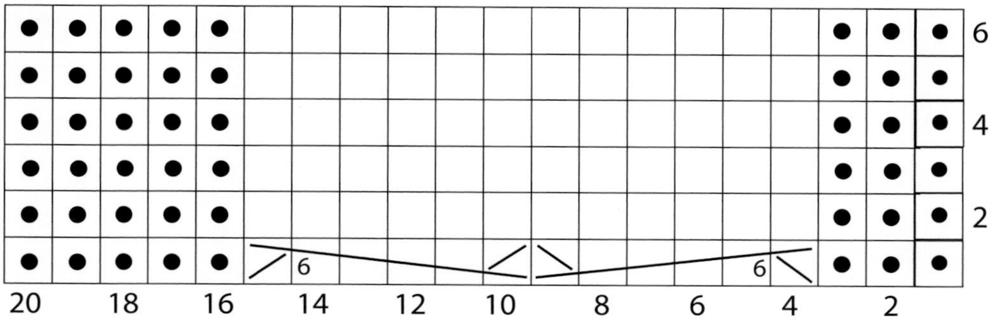
6
4
2
6
6
20
18
16
14
12
10
8
6
4
2

KEY

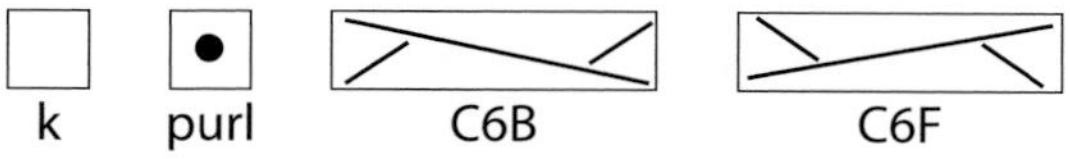
k
purl
C6B
C6F

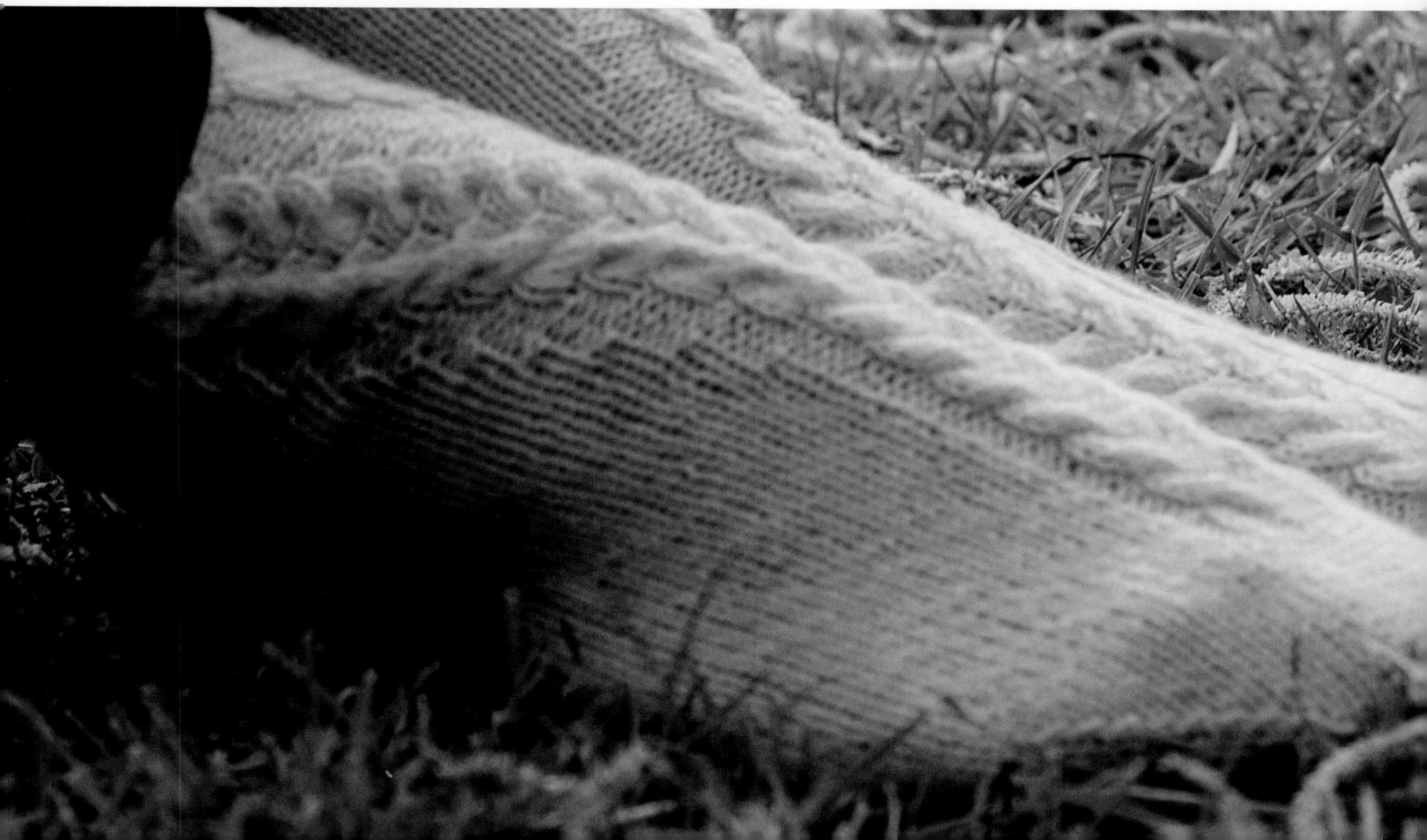

Eleanor

My knitting journey began in a tiny yarn shop in my home town, supported by the owner, who became one of my best friends. This fun yet beautiful design is lovingly dedicated to her. You don't need to be an experienced cable knitter, but be sure to keep tracks of your row counts as you knit.

Eleanor

Materials

1 skein of Unbelievawool sparkle sock in Just Lilac (75% superwash merino, 20% nylon, 5% stellina 400m per 100g)
2.5mm 9" mini circular needles or desired cable length for magic loop
stitch markers

Note: you may prefer to mirror the socks rather than knit two the same. To do this, on the second sock, work your cables to the front, rather than the back.

To begin:

CO 66 (72) using a long tail or cable cast on. Join in the round and place a stitch marker, taking care not to twist the stitches.

Ribbing:

* p1, k4, p1 (2), k4, p1 * repeat to end.
Repeat this row a total of 10 times

Reading from the bottom right hand corner of the chart, work row 1 and repeat it to the end of the round to establish pattern. Continue to work in chart, or follow the written instructions below.

Pattern:

R1: * p1, C4B, p1 (2), k4, p1 * repeat to end of round
R2: * p1, k4, p1 (2), k4, p1 * repeat to end of round
R3: as row 2
R4: as row 2
R5: as row 1
R6: * p1, k4, p1(2), C4B, p1 * repeat to end of round
R7: as row 2
R8: as row 2
R9: as row 2
R10: as row 6
R11: as row 2
R12: as row 2
R13: as row 2
R14: as row 6
R15: as row 2
R16: as row 2
R17: as row 2
R18: as row 2

Repeat the cable pattern at least three times on the leg before working the heel across 32 (36) st

For the heel:

TURN to work on the wrong side
WS: sl 1, p3, [k1 (2), p4, k2, p4] twice, k1 (2), p4, k1, turn
RS: sl 1, k4, [p1 (2), k4, p2, k4] twice, p1 (2), k4, turn,

Repeat these 2 rows a total of 16 times (32 rows) and the WS row once more so you finish with the RS row facing you.

To turn the heel,

With RS facing,
sl 1, k17 (19), ssk, k1 turn
p1, p6, p2tog, p1, turn

R1: sl 1, k to 1st before the the gap, ssk to close the gap, k1, turn
R2: sl 1, p to 1st before the gap, p2tog, p1, turn
Repeat R1 and 2 until you cannot decrease across the gap anymore & fin sh on a RS row.

Gusset:

NOTE: as you work the gusset, you will repeat row 18 a total of 10 times, followed by a full repeat of the pattern and then 10 repeats of row 18 only. Then repeat the full pattern once more.

Pick up and knit evenly along the left side of your heel flap, place marker and work row 18 of pattern across the instep, place marker, pick up and knit evenly down right side of heel flap. Knit to first marker

Knit a full round working row 18 of pattern across the instep.

R1: Knit row 18 pattern across instep, slip marker, k1, ssk, k to 3st before marker, k2tog, k1
R2: Knit a full round working row 18 of pattern across instep.

Continue working in pattern, repeating row 18 a further 6 times followed by the full pattern repeat until you have 66 (72) stitches in a full round.

Once you have worked a full pattern repeat, knit row 18 a total of 10 more times followed by another full pattern repeat.

Repeat row 18 until your foot is approx. 1.5 – 2inches less than the desired foot length.

For the toe:

Note: As you work the toe, (with the exception of the first three stitches after your marker and last 3 stitches before your marker) on the top of the foot, continue to purl the purl stitches so the rib continues right up to the Kitchener.

R1: k until 3 st before your fi st marker, k2tog, k1, slip marker
k1, ssk, k until 3 st before next marker, k2tog, k1, slip marker
k1, ssk, knit to end of round.
R2: Knit every stitch.

Repeat these two rows until you have 12 stitches between each marker and use Kitchener stitch to graft he toe closed.

Repeat for the second sock, sew in your ends and block gently.

Charts:

Small

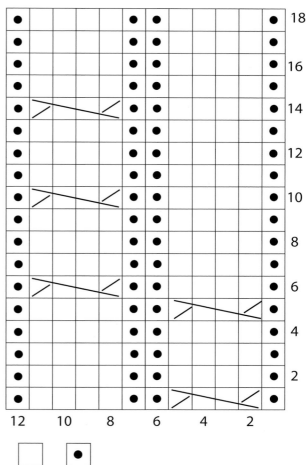
Large

Note: sock 2 reverses the cables

KEY

k   purl

C4B

Stitchionary

ws – wrong side

rs – right side

pm – place marker

sl m – slip marker

sl – slip stitch. Insert from left needle to right as if to purl

sl wyif – slip with yarn in front. Slip stitch from left to right needle while holding your working yarn in the front

k – knit

p – purl

yo – yarn over. Bring yarn over your right needle and return to the working position

Ktbl – knit through the back leg. Insert left hand needle into the back, rather than the front of the stitch on the right hand needle, and knit it. This creates a twisted stitch.

K2tog – knit two together. Insert the left hand needle into the next two stitches and knit them together dropping both off the needle.

p2tog – purl two together. Insert left needle into the front of the next two stitches, purl them both at the same time dropping both off the needle.

ssk – slip, slip, knit. Slip as if to purl, slip as if to knit, slip back onto left needle and knit together through the back

C4B – cable 4 in the back. Slip two stitches onto cable needle and hold to the back of your work. Knit two, then knit two from the cable needle

C4F - cable 4 in the front. Slip two stitches onto cable needle and hold to the front of your work. Knit two, then knit two from the cable needle

C6B - cable 6 in the back. Slip three stitches onto cable needle and hold to the back of your work. Knit three, then knit three from the cable needle

C6F - cable 6 in the front. Slip three stitches onto cable needle and hold to the front of your work. Knit three, then knit three from the cable needle

Chart Key

| k | ktbl | purl | yo | pattern repeat | ssk | k2tog | C4B | C4F | C6B | C6F |

Sock Sizes

All the patterns within this book contain the instruction 'knit foot until 1.5-2 inches less than desired length'. This point should be roughly in line with the base of your little toe. If you are knitting for someone else, the tables here may be useful to guide your knitting.

These measurements are the foot length taken from the back of the heel, to the tip of the big toe.

uk mens	inches
5	9
6	9.5
7	9.75
8	10
9	10.75
10	11
11	11.75
12	12

uk ladies	inches
3	8.75
4	9
5	9.25
6	9.75
7	10
8	10.25
9	10.75
10	11

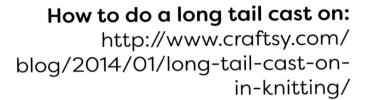

Resources

These are all great photo and video tutorials that may help you with elements of sock construction. There are lots available online though, so if you can't find these specific ones, don't be afraid to have a look around.

How to do a long tail cast on: http://www.craftsy.com/blog/2014/01/long-tail-cast-on-in-knitting/

How to do a cable cast on: https://www.youtube.com/watch?v=e4p6ybqnvVc

How to do a short row heel: http://happy-knits.blogspot.co.uk/2009/10/no-wrap-no-gap-short-row-heel-tutorial.html

How to do an Eye of Partridge heel: http://www.haveayarn.ca/stitch/03_2009_stitch_of_the_month.htm

How to do Kitchener stitch: http://www.knitty.com/ISSUE-summer04/FEATtheresasum04.html

Materials

Truly Hooked Hand Dyed Yarns
Available via www.trulyhooked.com
Also visit
www.facebook.com/trulyhooked for news of new
yarns, pattern releases and
show appearances.

Socks Yeah!
By www.coopknits.co.uk Also available from www.
knitnottingham.co.uk/shop

Bellica Yarns
Available from www.facebook.com/bellicayarns

HiyaHiya
For mini circular and cable needles, stitch markers
and other accessories Visit www.hiyahiya-europe.
com Also available from www.trulyhooked.com

Doodlestop
For stitch markers, yarn buddies and sock blockers
Visit www.doodlestop.co.uk
Easy Knits Visit www.easyknits.co.uk

Unbelievawool
Visit www.facebook.com/unbelievawool

Easy Knits
Visit www.easyknits.co.uk

Acknowledgements

Thank you, so very much to everyone who has helped this book come to life. You've all been hugely important to the process, no matter how small your part has been, and I'm eternally grateful.

My wonderful test knitters; I couldn't have done it without you! Your patience, skill, and feedback has been appreciated so much. A special thanks goes to Gemma for her speedy knitting when a wrist injury hindered my progress.

Thank you to my Mum, my family and my friends, both in real life and online, for their amazing support and encouragement in giving me the confidence to publish these designs. Thanks especially to Eleanor, who has been there from the first moment I put sticks to string and I will forever be indebted to her.

Thank you also to my Mum and Step Dad who allowed us to use their beautiful home for our photographs.

To my husband, Meyrick, who has also worked incredibly hard on this book; he deserves a page of thanks all to himself! From taking and editing photos, creating the charts, developing the layout and tolerating my relentless nagging, his contribution to the book has been phenomenal and I'm so proud of our joint accomplishment! Thank you for your limitless love and support, and for doing this with me.

Finally, I'd like to dedicate this book to my late Father, Paul, whose sudden death took my life in a new direction, and changed it in positive ways I could never have expected. I miss you every day.

About the Author.

Nottingham born Mother-of-two Verity is an award nominated
Independent yarn dyer and designer, with her knitting and
crochet patterns being published in popular magazines.
A lover of bright colours, her designs are simple to follow and
easy to adapt. She always has a project in her bag and loves
nothing more than an evening of knitting, accompanied by a
strong Gin and Tonic.

Other books also available:

On The Hook

The Second Drawer Down

On The Hook

Beautiful crochet patterns to expand your collection
by Verity Castledine

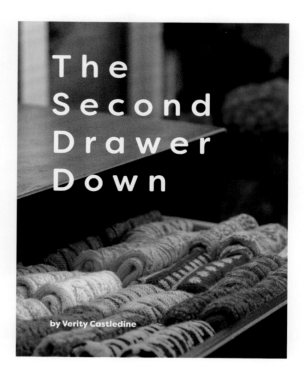

The Second Drawer Down

by Verity Castledine

The Sweater
That Lived

An enchanting knitting pattern by Verity Castledine

Now available on ravelry